Little Scientists ®

A "hands-on" approach to learning

Learning About the Way Things Move

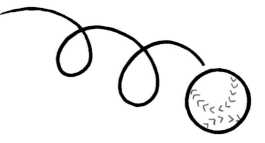

Dear Parents,

Young children are natural scientists, curious about the world around them. They have an infinite capacity to learn and are eager to know why and how things work the way they do. *Little Scientists, Hands-On Activities* begins with the simple questions most children ask and then shows them how to explore and find out for themselves. Our acclaimed Little Scientists, "hands-on" approach instills in children a passion for the exciting world of science and helps children develop specific scientific skills that will provide a strong foundation for later learning.

With this book, you can join me on a journey into the wonders of the way things move. Together we will discover the unlocked secrets of motion, and learn how to create paper airplanes, paper helicopters, and many other exciting things.

Your Little Scientist can email me at
Dr_Heidi@Little-Scientists.com

Wishing you success,

Dr. Heidi

Little Scientists®
A "hands-on" approach to learning

Learning About the Way Things Move

Heidi Gold-Dworkin, Ph.D.

McGraw-Hill

New York   San Francisco   Washington, D.C.
Auckland   Bogotá   Caracas   Lisbon   London   Madrid   Mexico City
Milan   Montreal   New Delhi   San Juan   Singapore   Sydney   Tokyo   Toronto

*This book is dedicated to my children
Aviva, Olivia, and Robert*

This book would not have been possible without the contributions
from the following staff members at Little Scientists:®
Ronda Margolis
Avi Ornstein
Linda Burian

I would like to thank my devoted family, especially
my husband, Jay; mom, Jacqueline; and sister, Stacey.

McGraw-Hill

A Division of The **McGraw-Hill** *Companies*

pbk   2 3 4 5 6 7 8 9 0 QPD / QPD 0 9 8 7 6 5 4 3 2 1 0

ISBN 0-07-134824-7

Library of Congress Cataloging-in-Publication data applied for.

McGraw-Hill books are available at special quantity discounts to use as premiums
and sales promotions. For more information, please write to the Director of Special Sales,
McGraw-Hill, Two Penn Plaza, New York, NY 10121-2298. Or contact your local bookstore.

Acquisitions editor: Mary Loebig Giles
Senior editing supervisor: Patricia V. Amoroso
Senior production supervisors: Clare B. Stanley and Charles Annis
Left page illustrations: Robert K. Ullman <r.k.ullman@worldnet.att.net>
Right page illustrations: K. Almadingen <dzbersin@aol.com>
Book design: Jaclyn J. Boone <bookdesign@rcn.com>

Printed and bound by Quebecor/Dubuque.

This book is printed on recycled, acid-free paper containing
a minimum of 50% recycled, de-inked fiber.

Contents

Hi, I'm Dr. Heidi.
Let's follow my Little Scientists® friends, Robbie, Olivia, and Aviva,
as they discover the many different forces that affect the way
things move. You'll be able to follow my directions and
do your own experiments to study these forces, too!

Why does everything always come back down?

Gravity is a force that is all around us, pulling down everything, including us. Long ago, a scientist named Galileo tested to see if gravity affects different objects in the same way. He dropped two balls — one heavy and one light — from the Leaning Tower of Pisa in Italy. Try this experiment and see what happens!

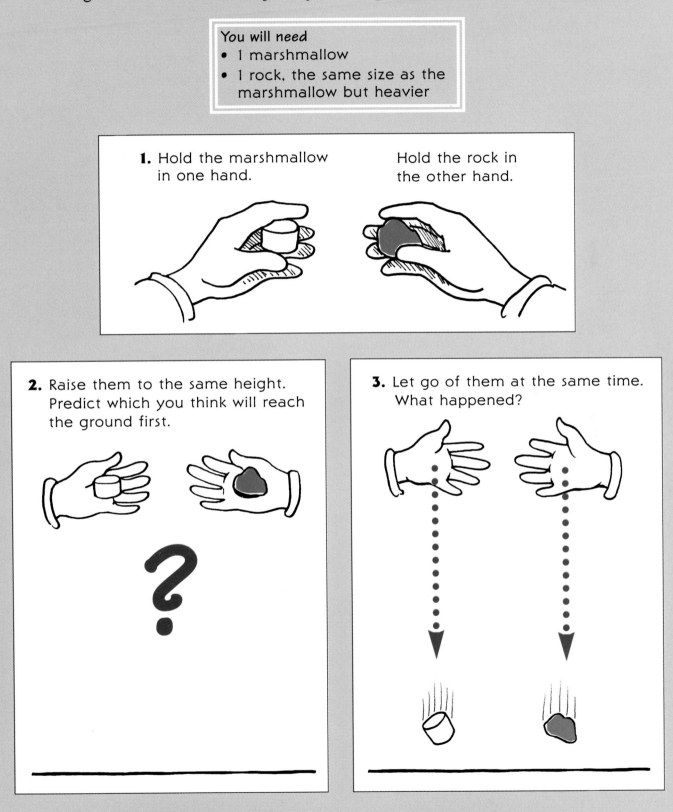

You will need
- 1 marshmallow
- 1 rock, the same size as the marshmallow but heavier

1. Hold the marshmallow in one hand.

Hold the rock in the other hand.

2. Raise them to the same height. Predict which you think will reach the ground first.

?

3. Let go of them at the same time. What happened?

Both objects should reach the ground at the same time.

Why are some things so hard to lift?

Size is not important. The important factor is weight, which depends on gravity. The more something weighs, the more you're fighting gravity when you try to lift it. That's why it is harder to lift heavy things. Let's test this out.

1. Select an item and try to lift it.

You will need
- Bathroom scale
- Variety of items
  - large book,
  - bag of potatoes,
  - bag of marshmallows,
  - plant in a flowerpot,
  - large can of food,
  - big rock,
  - soda bottle,
  - your shoes

2. Guess how much it weighs.

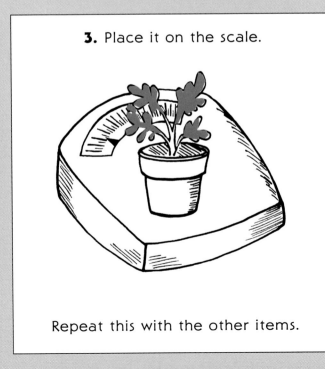

3. Place it on the scale.

See how well you can predict weight by seeing how difficult it is to lift something.

Repeat this with the other items.

Does gravity pull everything the same way?

Let's find out if all things are pulled by gravity at the same speed.

You will need
• 2 sheets of 8 1/2" x 11" paper

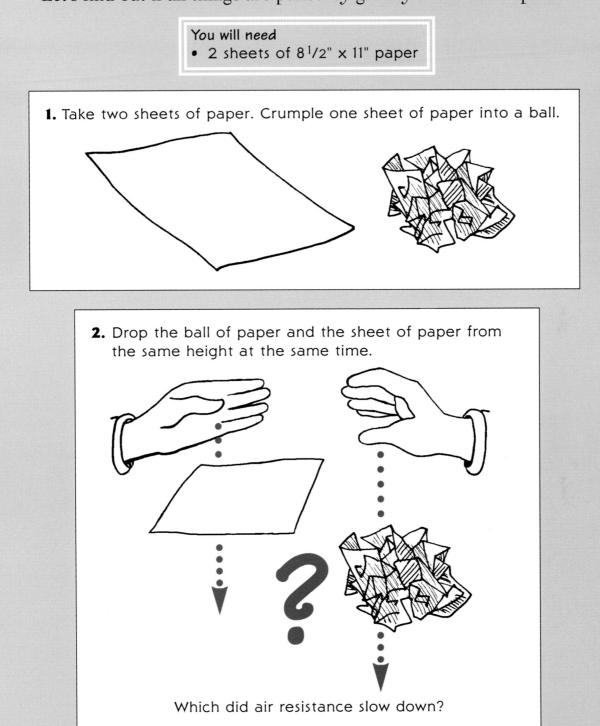

1. Take two sheets of paper. Crumple one sheet of paper into a ball.

2. Drop the ball of paper and the sheet of paper from the same height at the same time.

Which did air resistance slow down?

In the experiment, the flat sheet of paper and the crumpled sheet had the same weight. Gravity pulled both sheets of paper at the same speed, but there was another force! If you wave your hand in the air, you can feel **air resistance** as you push the air out of the way. When you dropped the flat sheet of paper, the air resistance was greater because the area of the paper was larger — more air had to be pushed out of the way for the sheet of paper to fall. That's why it fell slower.

When leaves fall from trees, they float to the ground.
This is due to air resistance. Air resistance is air pushing against moving objects.
Parachutes use air resistance so people jumping out of planes do not fall too quickly.
Let's make a simple parachute and see how it slows down a falling object!

1. Hold up the small plastic toy and then let go of it. Observe how quickly it falls to the ground.

You will need
- Small plastic toy (1" to 2" high)
- Tape
- 12" x 12" sheet of tissue paper
- 4 lengths of 18" thread

2. Tape one length of thread to each of the four corners of the tissue paper.

3. Pull the four threads together and tie them to the plastic toy.

4. Use both hands to spread out the tissue paper with the toy hanging below.

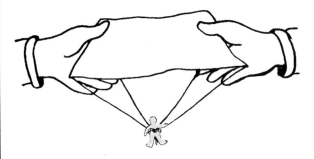

5. Pull your hands to the side, letting go of your parachute. Observe how the toy falls to the ground.

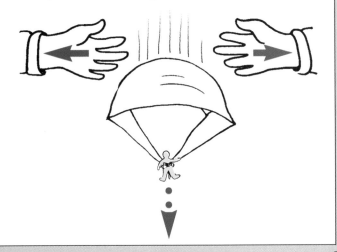

If gravity is always pulling
everything down, how can we stand?
Why don't we fall down?

Things can stay standing as long as there is support under the point called the **center of gravity**! Let's see what happens when you try this with your own body. Your body is not a simple shape, but somewhere inside you is your center of gravity. If you keep your center of gravity over your feet, you will be able to stand. But if the center of gravity isn't over your feet...

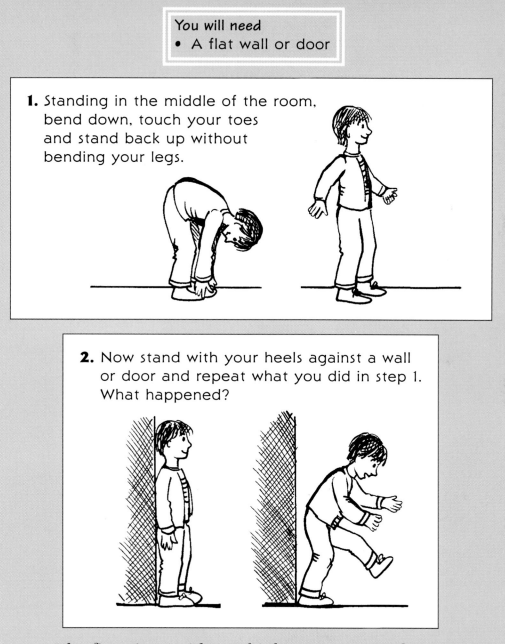

You will *need*
• A flat wall or door

1. Standing in the middle of the room, bend down, touch your toes and stand back up without bending your legs.

2. Now stand with your heels against a wall or door and repeat what you did in step 1. What happened?

The first time, without thinking, you moved your body to keep your center of gravity over your feet. Repeat what you did the first time and see how you change the position of your body — part of your body goes back to keep your center of gravity over your feet! The second time, the wall or door was in the way. Your center of gravity could not stay over your feet and gravity pulled you down!

What makes some balls go faster than others?

When things are moving, they stay at the same speed unless some force pushes or pulls them. If there is a force, they can speed up. This is called **acceleration**! Sometimes it is hard to recognize when something is accelerating. You have to observe very carefully while doing this experiment.

> **You will need**
> • Small, soft ball

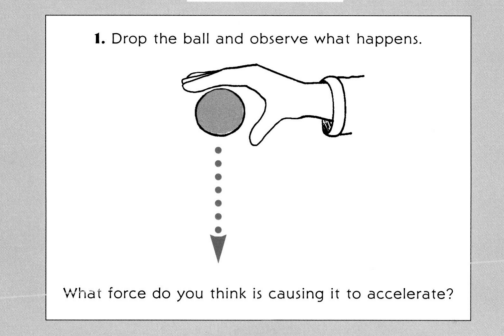

1. Drop the ball and observe what happens.

What force do you think is causing it to accelerate?

2. Now toss the ball up and pay special attention as you watch what happens.

It was very hard to notice, but the ball went faster as it fell. The force that caused it to accelerate was gravity. When you tossed it up, it should have been easier to notice the effect. Gravity was always making it accelerate downward. First it slowed down the ball's upward motion and then it sped up its downward motion!

Why does the ball keep moving?

When something is falling, it keeps going until it hits the ground.
A ball sitting on the ground will not move by itself. This is another force,
called **inertia**. Inertia means that, unless some other force is added,
moving things will keep moving and things that are not moving will stay still.
Let's test this out!

1. Place the ball on the ground.

You will need
• Hard, plastic ball

2. See if you can make it move
without applying any force
directly to the ball, such as
touching the ball or blowing it.
For example, try telling the
ball to move. What happens?

MOVE

3. Roll the ball on the floor. If it stops moving,
see if you can discover what force
caused it to stop.

Without applying some force, you couldn't get the ball to move.
When the rolling ball stopped, there was some force making it stop.
Maybe it hit a wall, which pushed against it. Maybe it rubbed
against the floor. When you finish the activities in this book,
it should be easier for you to explain why the ball stopped.

Why are wheels round?

In this experiment, you will compare different shapes to see which rolls the best.

1. Slightly flatten one of the toilet paper tubes so that it is oval shaped.

You will need
- 2 cardboard toilet paper tubes
- Long box (like a toothpaste box)
- Toy figurine
- Several kinds of fruit (grape, lemon, apple, and banana)
- Different shaped blocks

2. Roll both tubes along a table. Which do you think rolls more easily?

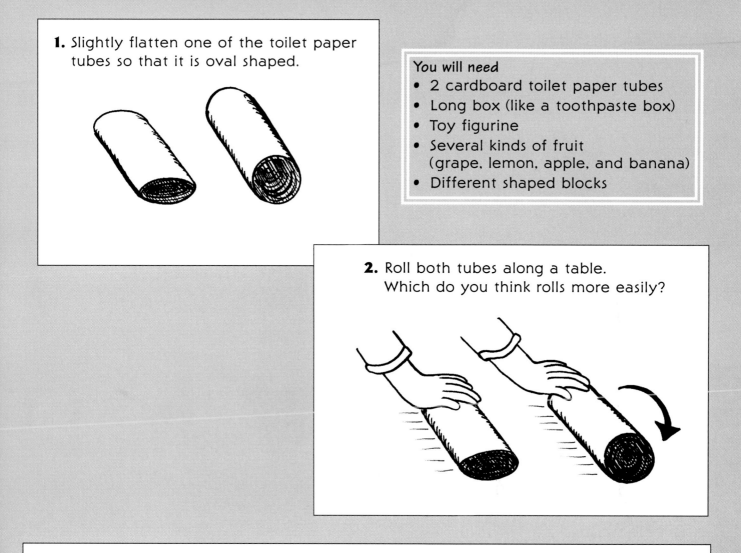

3. Take one object at a time and try rolling it and the round tube on the table.

Which is the easiest to roll? Which is the most difficult?

Wheels are round because that is the shape that moves the best.

Why do wheels work so well?

Because wheels are round, only a small spot — a thin line across the bottom of the wheel — touches the ground at any one time. As that spot pushes against the ground, friction makes the wheels turn and they roll along. Let's find out how wheels move in this experiment. Carefully watch the book and pencils to see what happens.

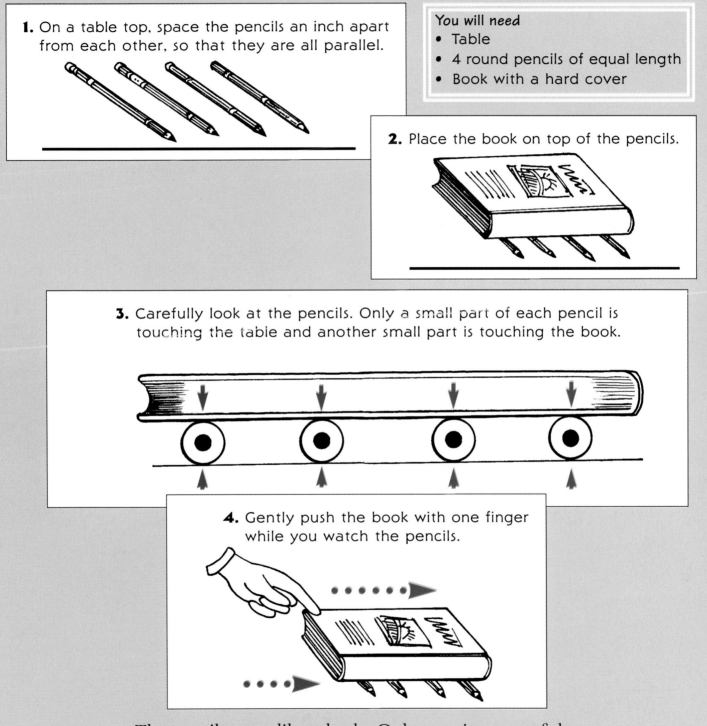

1. On a table top, space the pencils an inch apart from each other, so that they are all parallel.

You will need
- Table
- 4 round pencils of equal length
- Book with a hard cover

2. Place the book on top of the pencils.

3. Carefully look at the pencils. Only a small part of each pencil is touching the table and another small part is touching the book.

4. Gently push the book with one finger while you watch the pencils.

The pencils were like wheels. Only one tiny part of the surface of the pencil touched the table at one time. The book actually rolled over the pencils. Many people think the Egyptians moved heavy rocks over round objects to build the pyramids!

This wagon works great!

The wagon works great because of the wheels, but wheels by themselves are not enough. Let's do an experiment to see if this is true.

1. Punch a hole in the middle of one end of an index card and tie a string to it.

You will *need*
- Index card
- Hole punch
- String
- 4 pieces of wagon wheel-shaped pasta

2. Stand the four pieces of wagon wheel pasta in the same positions as the wheels on a car.

3. Try to put the index card on top of the pasta.
What happens when you pull it?
What happens to the wheels?

Just having wheels didn't work.
When you pulled the card, the wheels were left behind!

What is holding
the wheels
together?

22

The wheels are attached in a special way. Both sets of wheels were attached to each other with a bar called an **axle**. An axle is necessary for the wheels to work together. It also attaches the wheels to the wagon or car. You can see how wheels and axles work by making them on your own.

You will need
- Hole punch
- Index card
- String
- Safety scissors
- Drinking straw
- 4 pieces of wagon wheel–shaped pasta
- 2 pieces of straight ziti pasta
- Tape

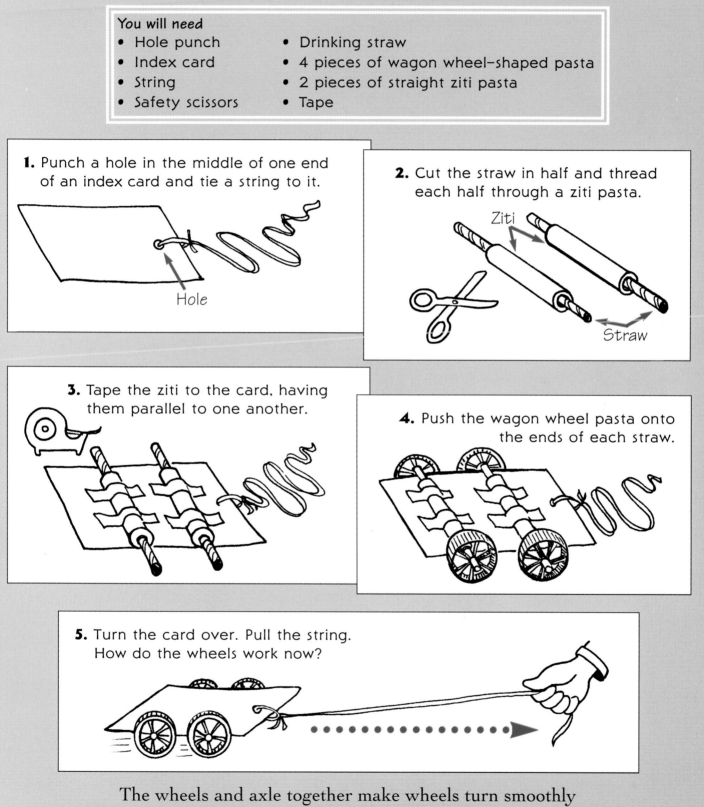

1. Punch a hole in the middle of one end of an index card and tie a string to it.

Hole

2. Cut the straw in half and thread each half through a ziti pasta.

Ziti

Straw

3. Tape the ziti to the card, having them parallel to one another.

4. Push the wagon wheel pasta onto the ends of each straw.

5. Turn the card over. Pull the string. How do the wheels work now?

The wheels and axle together make wheels turn smoothly and make the wagon, car, or roller skates work.

Why is it hard to move my wagon
when the ground is bumpy?

It is hard for Robbie to move his wagon because it is on a rough surface. Test for yourself to see how friction (one object rubbing against another) affects motion.

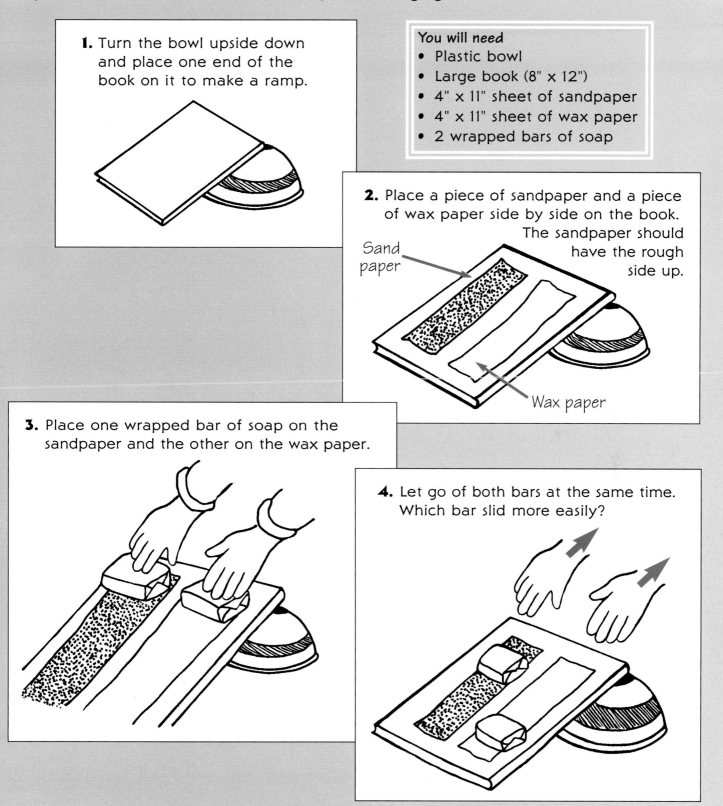

1. Turn the bowl upside down and place one end of the book on it to make a ramp.

You will need
- Plastic bowl
- Large book (8" x 12")
- 4" x 11" sheet of sandpaper
- 4" x 11" sheet of wax paper
- 2 wrapped bars of soap

2. Place a piece of sandpaper and a piece of wax paper side by side on the book. The sandpaper should have the rough side up.

Sand paper

Wax paper

3. Place one wrapped bar of soap on the sandpaper and the other on the wax paper.

4. Let go of both bars at the same time. Which bar slid more easily?

It is much harder to move on the sandpaper because of the increased friction. The rough bumps on the sandpaper catch on the surface of anything moving over them. **Friction** is a force that can make it harder to move.

25

Too little friction
is also a problem!

You can't move when there is too much friction. But if you don't have any friction, your feet will slip and you also won't move! Let's look at what happens when you take away friction. (Don't try this on a smooth floor. You could easily fall down!)

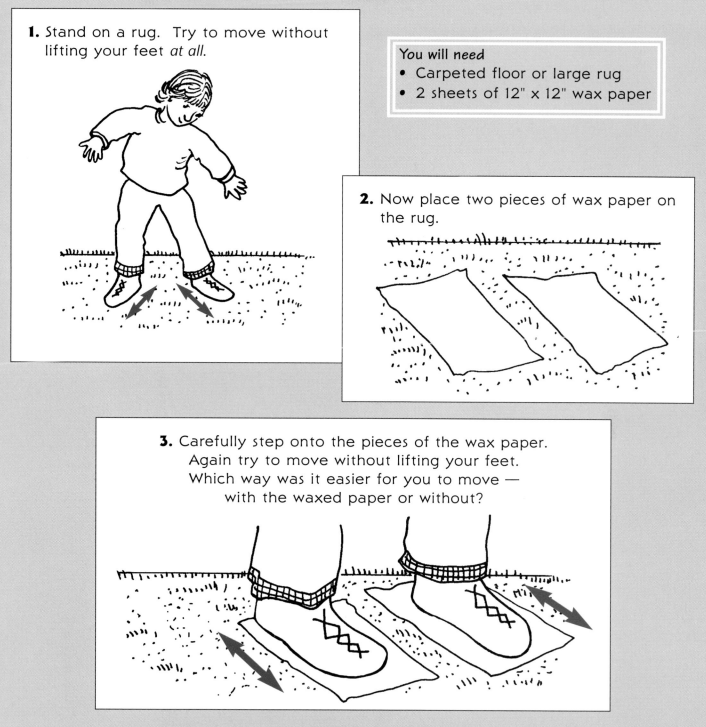

1. Stand on a rug. Try to move without lifting your feet *at all.*

You will need
- Carpeted floor or large rug
- 2 sheets of 12" x 12" wax paper

2. Now place two pieces of wax paper on the rug.

3. Carefully step onto the pieces of the wax paper. Again try to move without lifting your feet. Which way was it easier for you to move — with the waxed paper or without?

In the first case, there was too much friction on the rug.
Your feet pressed against the rug and the rough surfaces kept you where you were.
In the second case, the wax paper made a smooth surface between your feet and the rug.
You were able to slide your feet without lifting them!
If there were no friction, you wouldn't be able to stay standing — or even sit in a chair!

What is pressure?

Pressure is another force.
Pressure plays a part whenever a ball bounces. Pressure depends upon both how hard you push and the area against which you are pressing. Let's do an experiment to see how **surface area** — the amount of space where two objects are touching each other — affects pressure.

1. Place the box on a table so that it is against a wall.

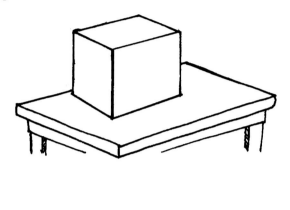

You will **need**
- Corrugated cardboard box
- Table and wall
- Sharpened pencil

2. Make a fist with one hand and hold the pencil in your other hand.

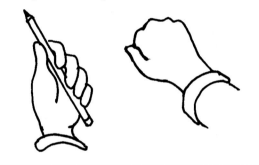

3. Gently place both the tip of the pencil and your fist against the box.

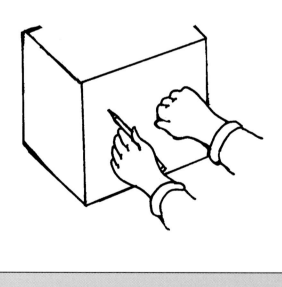

4. Push both the pencil tip and your fist against the box as hard as you can. What happened? Did the pencil pierce the box? What about your fist?

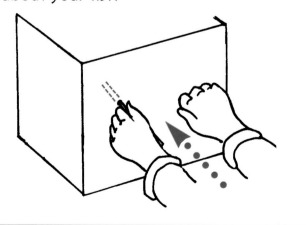

You are not stronger than yourself, so you are comparing the pressure of a small area (the tip of the pencil) to the pressure of a larger area (the surface of your fist). When the area is smaller, the pressure is greater. While the cardboard was strong enough to stop your fist, the pressure at the tip of the pencil was great enough to push through the cardboard.

Why is it harder
to push some things?

Some substances can be **compressed** — they can be squeezed into smaller spaces. Some cannot. Some can be **displaced** — they move out of the way. Some cannot. Let's experiment to discover whether liquids, gases, and solids can be compressed and displaced.

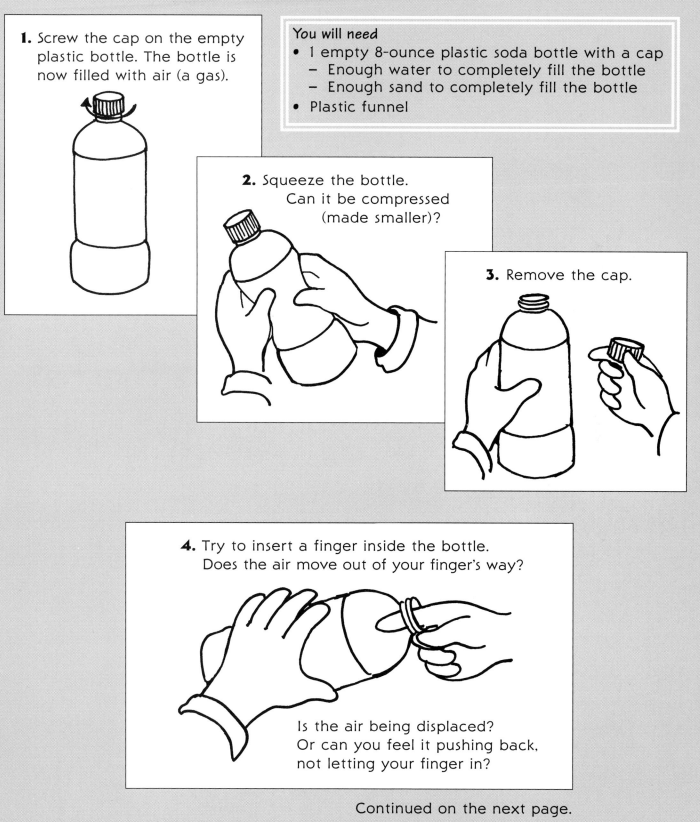

1. Screw the cap on the empty plastic bottle. The bottle is now filled with air (a gas).

You will need
- 1 empty 8-ounce plastic soda bottle with a cap
  - Enough water to completely fill the bottle
  - Enough sand to completely fill the bottle
- Plastic funnel

2. Squeeze the bottle. Can it be compressed (made smaller)?

3. Remove the cap.

4. Try to insert a finger inside the bottle. Does the air move out of your finger's way?

Is the air being displaced? Or can you feel it pushing back, not letting your finger in?

Continued on the next page.

5. Fill the bottle all the way up to the top with water (a liquid).

Screw the cap back on tightly.

6. Squeeze the bottle.

Can it be compressed?

7. Remove the lid.

8. Try to insert a finger inside the bottle. Can the water be displaced?

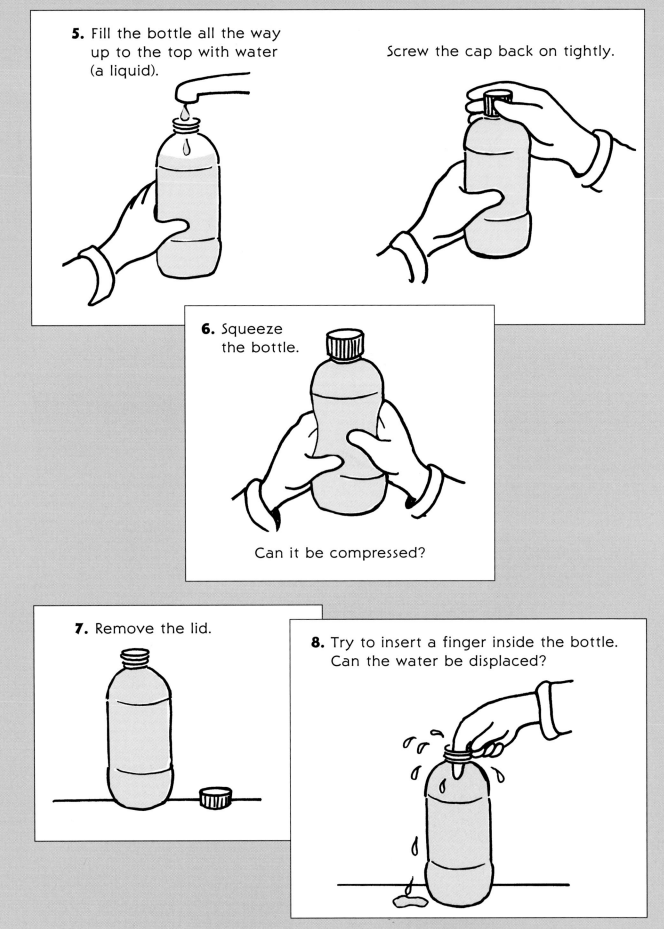

Continued on the next page.

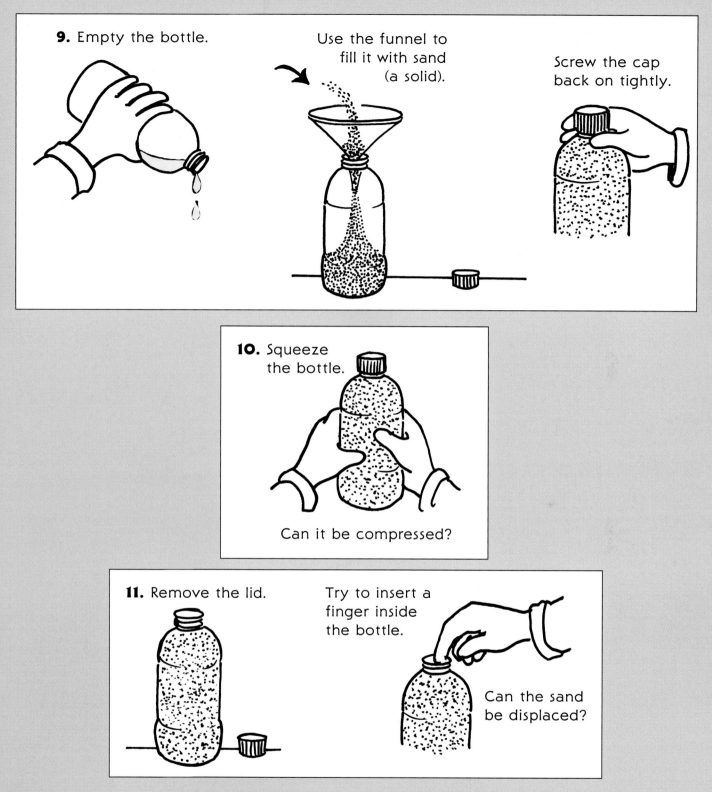

9. Empty the bottle.

Use the funnel to fill it with sand (a solid).

Screw the cap back on tightly.

10. Squeeze the bottle.

Can it be compressed?

11. Remove the lid.

Try to insert a finger inside the bottle.

Can the sand be displaced?

You should have had a different set of results for each type of matter. Gases, such as air, can be both compressed and displaced. You could squeeze the bottle a bit and you could insert your finger. The molecules can move closer together and they are free to move out of the way. Liquids, such as water, can be displaced, but they cannot be compressed. The molecules are free to move around, but they cannot move closer together. Solids, such as sand, can neither be compressed nor can they be displaced.

Is air pressure a real force?

The air pressure of the atmosphere always presses against your body. It is very strong, but you don't feel it since the pressure inside your body pushes out with the same force. Since it is invisible and we do not feel it directly, you have to be a very good scientist if you want to do experiments to learn about it. You have to observe carefully and be ready for anything.
Let's see what happens when the pressures are not equal.

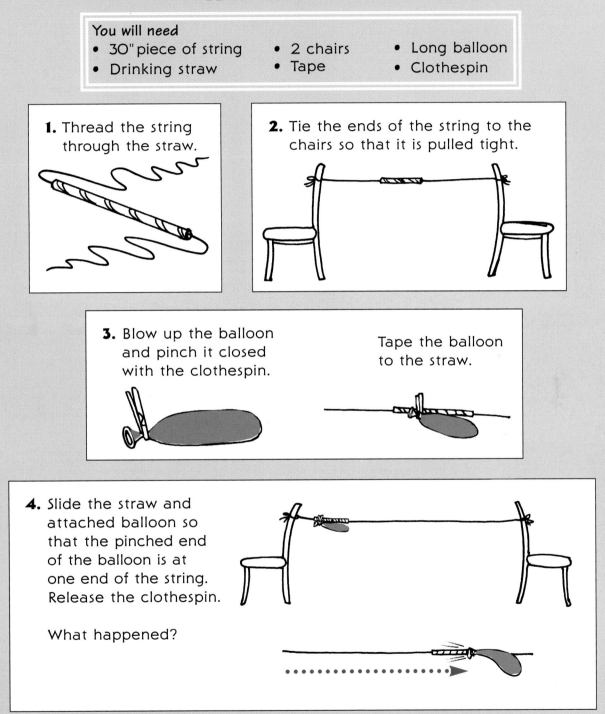

You will need
- 30" piece of string
- Drinking straw
- 2 chairs
- Tape
- Long balloon
- Clothespin

1. Thread the string through the straw.

2. Tie the ends of the string to the chairs so that it is pulled tight.

3. Blow up the balloon and pinch it closed with the clothespin.

Tape the balloon to the straw.

4. Slide the straw and attached balloon so that the pinched end of the balloon is at one end of the string. Release the clothespin.

What happened?

The atmosphere pressed against the outside of the balloon and the air inside the balloon was pushed out. The balloon and straw moved in the other direction!

If there is no wind,
is there still air pressure?

Air pressure is different from wind. Air pressure is present even when the air is staying still. The air is always pushing — up, down, and sideways! Let's do another experiment to see if the pressure is really present.

You will need
- Clear glass
- Water
- Straw

1. Fill the glass 3/4 of the way with water.

2. Drop the straw in the glass.

3. Cover the top opening of the straw with one finger.

4. Lift up the straw. What is trapped inside the straw?

5. What happens when you remove your finger from the top of the straw?

Air was pushing up at the bottom of the straw, but your finger blocked the top of the straw. Air pressure was keeping the water inside the straw! When you removed your finger, air was pushing both up and down while gravity pulled the water down. That is why the water came out.

Can air pressure hurt me?

The water in the straw in the previous activity didn't show you how strong the air pressure is. The air pushing against us would crush us if we didn't have the same pressure inside our bodies pushing out. Let's try another experiment.

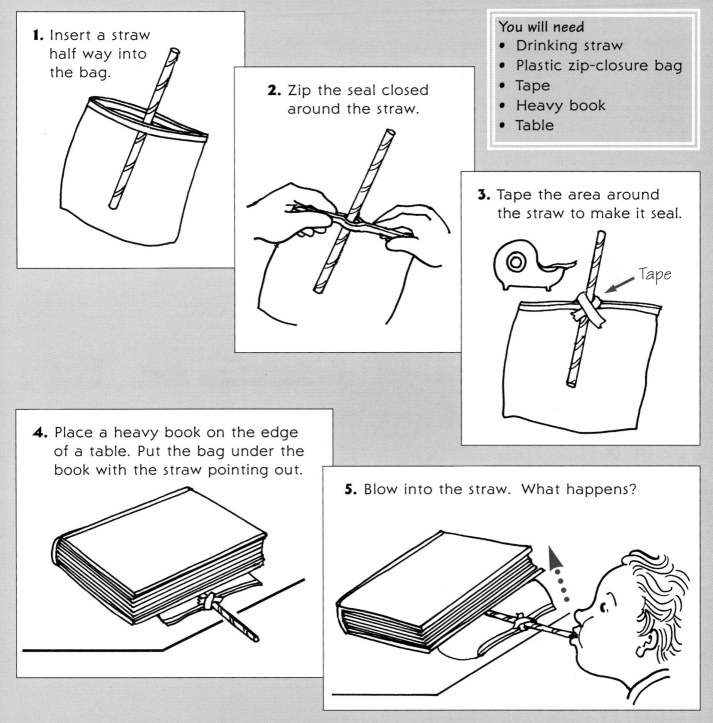

1. Insert a straw half way into the bag.

2. Zip the seal closed around the straw.

You will need
- Drinking straw
- Plastic zip-closure bag
- Tape
- Heavy book
- Table

3. Tape the area around the straw to make it seal.

Tape

4. Place a heavy book on the edge of a table. Put the bag under the book with the straw pointing out.

5. Blow into the straw. What happens?

The air blown into the bag increased the pressure and filled the bag so that it could lift the book. This would work even if the book was much heavier! Air pressure is very strong. Whenever you hold something up, you are winning a strength competition against gravity. If something is too heavy to lift, gravity is winning. At sea level, the air pressure pushing against an area of only one square inch is almost 15 pounds!

When air is moving, does the air pressure change?

Let's do an experiment to see how pressure is affected by moving air.

You will need
• 2 sheets of 8 1/2" x 11" paper

1. Grasp each sheet of paper in the middle of one edge, holding each one between the thumb and index finger of each hand.

2. Hold the sheets so that they are facing each other and are at eye level, but not touching your face.

3. Blow air between the two sheets to push them farther apart.

What happened?

Were you surprised that the sheets moved together?
When air moves, the air pressure decreases.
The air between the sheets was moving, so it had less
pressure than the air on the outside surface of each sheet.

How can a plane stay in the sky, if gravity pulls all things down?

Moving air causes an upward force called **lift**. This is what keeps an airplane up in the sky. Daniel Bernoulli discovered this force caused by moving air, so it is called the **Bernoulli effect**. This force is being applied any time someone flies in a plane!

You will need
- 1" x 8" strip of paper

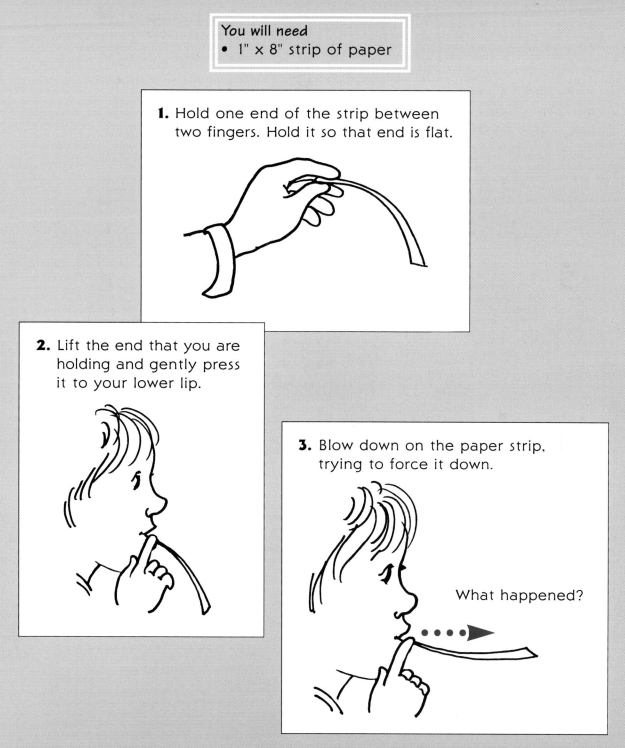

1. Hold one end of the strip between two fingers. Hold it so that end is flat.

2. Lift the end that you are holding and gently press it to your lower lip.

3. Blow down on the paper strip, trying to force it down.

What happened?

Before you blew any air, equal air pressure was pushing down and up against the paper strip. When you blew against the paper, you were making the air above the strip move. Air pressure decreases when air moves, so the pressure above the strip was less than the pressure below the strip. That is why the paper strip moved up.

Is the shape of a wing important?

The shape of a wing determines how fast air moves over it.
This air can't push down as hard as the air underneath pushes up.
When a new plane wing is designed, engineers make an **airfoil**,
which is a section of the wing. They test it in a wind tunnel to see
how much lift it has. Let's make an airfoil and test it for lift!

You will need
- 6" x 2" thick paper
- Ruler
- Tape
- Help from an adult
- 16" long thread
- Needle

1. Fold the paper length wise about 2 1/2 inches from one end.

2 1/2 inches

2. Tape the ends of the paper so the top has a curve and the bottom is flat.

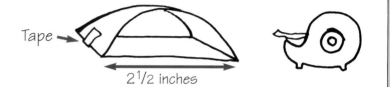

Tape →

2 1/2 inches

3. Have an adult thread the needle and push the needle through both layers of the wing, about one-third of the way from the folded edge.

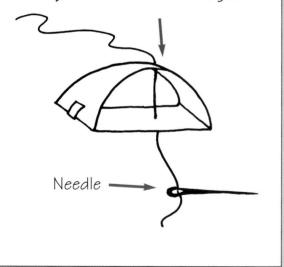

Needle →

4. Remove the needle from the thread. Slide the wing so that it is in the middle of the thread. Hold the ends of the thread so that the string goes up and down.

Blow at the folded edge of the wing. What happens?

What you made is called an airfoil. If you look sideways at the airfoil,
you can see that the bottom is flat and the top is curved. Air going over the airfoil
will have to go faster to reach the other end, as it must go a farther distance.
The downward pressure was less than the upward pressure.

How can I
make a plane
that flies?

By following these directions, you can make
a paper plane that can fly a long distance.

You will need
- 8 1/2" x 11" sheet of paper

1. Fold the sheet in half the long way and open it. This gives you a crease line.

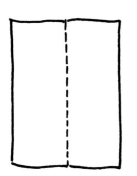

2. Fold one corner over to the crease line. Do the same for the corner closest to it.

Fold → ← Fold

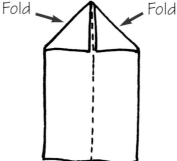

3. Take the folded edges and again fold each of them over to the crease.

Fold → ← Fold

4. For a third time, fold the folded edges to the crease line. The tip will be very pointed.

Fold → ← Fold

5. Turn the paper over and fold it in half on the crease line.

Crease →

6. Turn it back over and press down the flaps on each side, leaving the middle rib up.

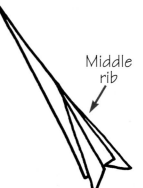

Middle rib

7. Go outside or into a large room. Hold the middle of the rib and throw the plane forward and slightly upward.

You have made a paper plane called a Dart.
With neat folds and firm creases your plane should fly far.
Practice throwing it, testing which way makes it go farther.

Why do we need seat belts?

Seat belts are very important!
Let's use your paper plane to test this out.

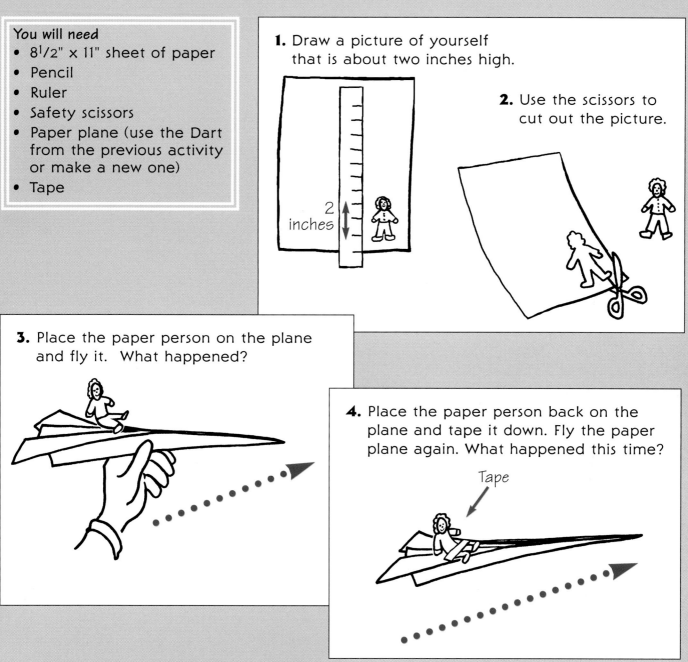

You will need
- 8¹/2" x 11" sheet of paper
- Pencil
- Ruler
- Safety scissors
- Paper plane (use the Dart from the previous activity or make a new one)
- Tape

1. Draw a picture of yourself that is about two inches high.

2 inches

2. Use the scissors to cut out the picture.

3. Place the paper person on the plane and fly it. What happened?

4. Place the paper person back on the plane and tape it down. Fly the paper plane again. What happened this time?

Tape

We saw another example of inertia in this activity.
When the paper person was not attached, it wanted to stay still
when the plane was flown. When it was taped in place, however,
it went with the plane and kept moving as long as the plane was moving.
The tape acted like a seat belt!

Whenever you are in a moving vehicle — whether it is a plane or a car —
you should always fasten your seat belt. If you are not wearing a seat belt
in a car and there is an accident, you will keep moving (because of inertia)
and you can be badly hurt.

Can I control how my paper plane flies?

Let's make a different paper plane. You can change both the wing flaps and how the weight is positioned. See how that changes the way the plane flies!

You will *need*
- 8¹/₂" x 11" sheet of paper
- Paper clip

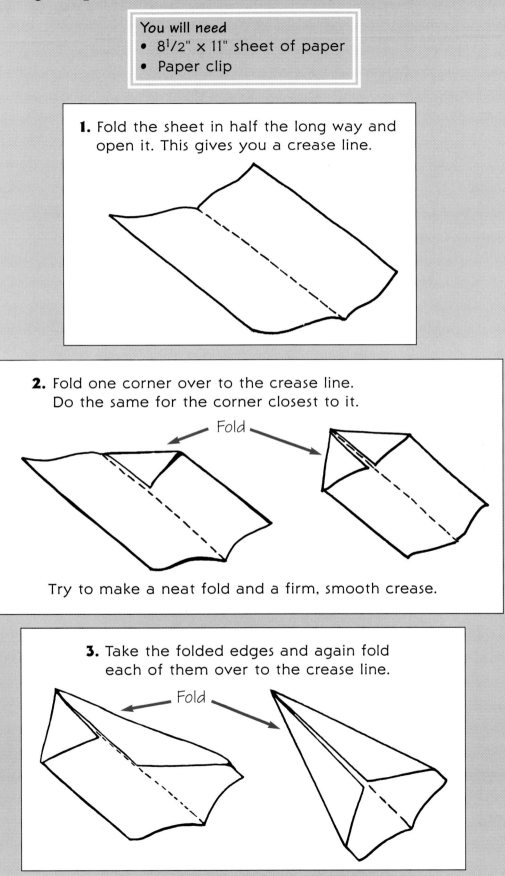

1. Fold the sheet in half the long way and open it. This gives you a crease line.

2. Fold one corner over to the crease line. Do the same for the corner closest to it.

Fold

Try to make a neat fold and a firm, smooth crease.

3. Take the folded edges and again fold each of them over to the crease line.

Fold

Continued on the next page.

4. Fold the paper back in half on the original crease line.

Fold →

5. Fold one side down an inch from the crease line fold.

Fold

6. Turn it over and fold the other side the same way.

Fold

7. Fold both sides halfway up. They are the plane's wings.

Fold

8. Attach a paper clip to the bottom on the plane's rib. You can choose where you want the paper clip to be.

Paper clip ←

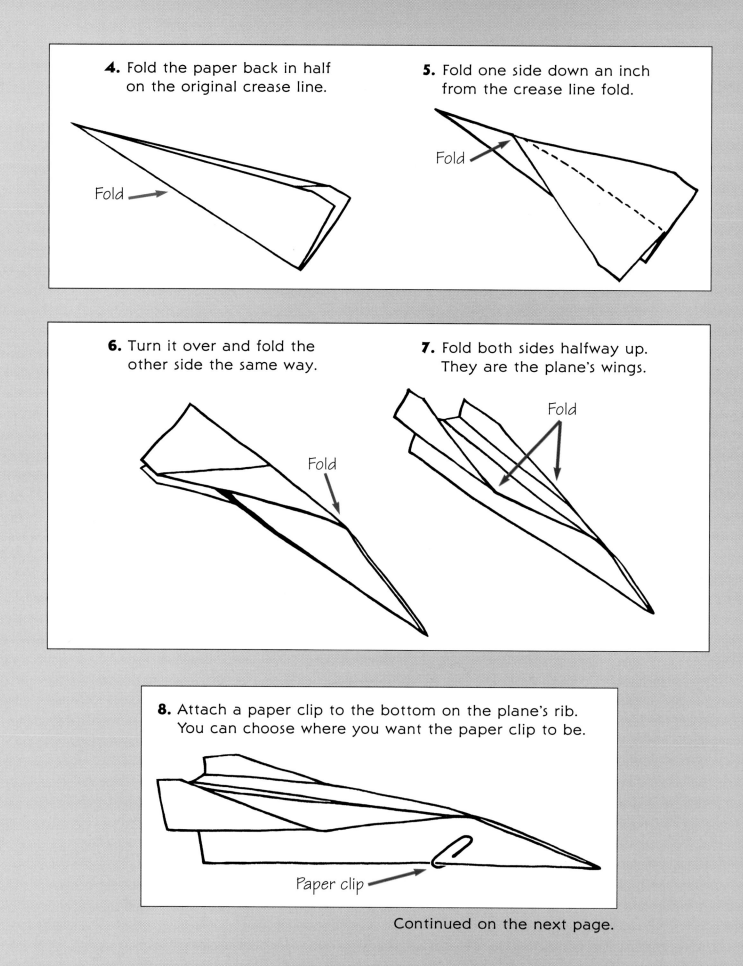

Continued on the next page.

9. Fold small flaps up or down at the end of each wing. You choose whether they go up or down — or you can choose to have no flaps.

Flaps

10. See how your plane flies. You can then change the angle of the flaps or how far forward or back the paper clip is positioned. Which way makes the plane fly the farthest?

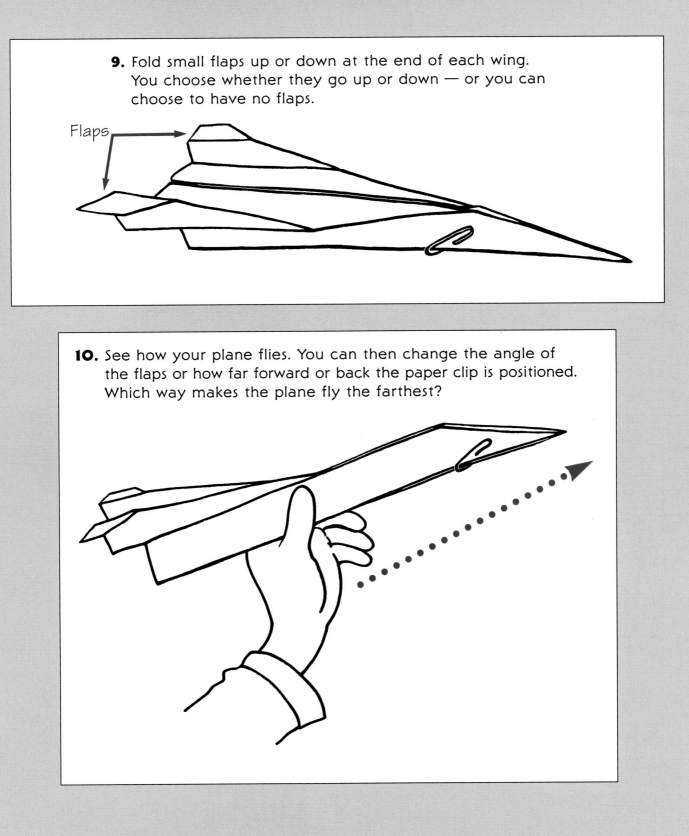

What makes a helicopter
different than a plane?

The spinning of the helicopter blade can create lift. A helicopter looks very different from an airplane, but the same force is keeping it in the air. The blades can make the helicopter go up and they can let it come down slowly.

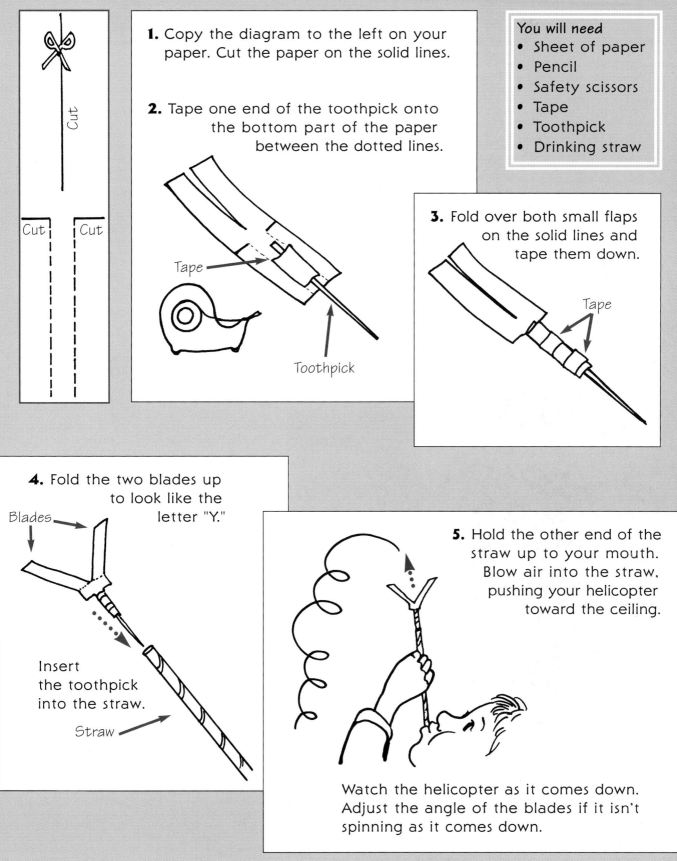

Cut

Cut   Cut

1. Copy the diagram to the left on your paper. Cut the paper on the solid lines.

2. Tape one end of the toothpick onto the bottom part of the paper between the dotted lines.

Tape

Toothpick

You will *need*
- Sheet of paper
- Pencil
- Safety scissors
- Tape
- Toothpick
- Drinking straw

3. Fold over both small flaps on the solid lines and tape them down.

Tape

4. Fold the two blades up to look like the letter "Y."

Blades

Insert the toothpick into the straw.

Straw

5. Hold the other end of the straw up to your mouth. Blow air into the straw, pushing your helicopter toward the ceiling.

Watch the helicopter as it comes down. Adjust the angle of the blades if it isn't spinning as it comes down.

How can a Frisbee® fly so well?

Another force affects spinning objects.
When something is spinning, it does not want to tilt.
Let's experiment to see how spin affects the flight of a Frisbee.®

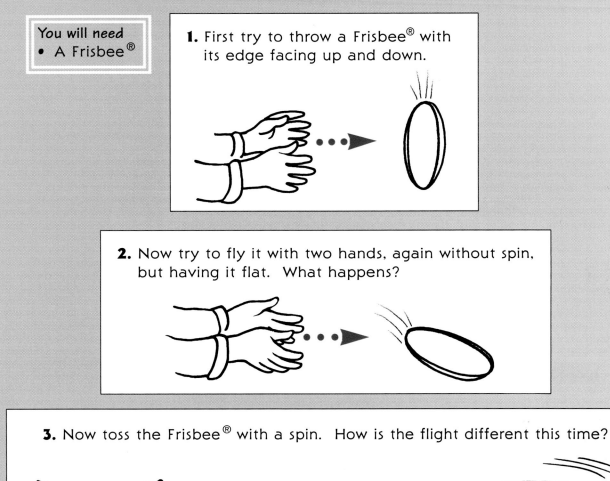

You will need
• A Frisbee®

1. First try to throw a Frisbee® with its edge facing up and down.

2. Now try to fly it with two hands, again without spin, but having it flat. What happens?

3. Now toss the Frisbee® with a spin. How is the flight different this time?

In the first case, it didn't fly well because the air stopped it very quickly. In the second case, the edge caught against the air, tipping it up so the air resistance again stopped it. In the last case, the motion caused by the spin kept it from tilting, allowing it to go much farther through the air.

This same force also applies to bicycles. When the bicycle wheels are spinning faster, it is easier to keep the bicycle balanced because the wheels don't want to tilt sideways!

Although this is the last experiment in this book, keep observing what is happening around you. Test things out by doing your own experiments. Maybe you'll even discover something new!

Glossary

acceleration — increase in speed — to scientists, it actually is any change in speed, either positive acceleration or negative acceleration (which is slowing down or deceleration)

adhesion — the sticking together of two different materials caused by an attraction between molecules

air pressure — pressure due to air molecules colliding with one another and the surrounding surfaces

air resistance — air molecules collide with a moving object and cause it to slow down

Bernoulli effect — named after Daniel Bernoulli. The fact that air pressure decreases when air is moving

buoyancy — the ability to float in a given liquid or gas

center of gravity — the midpoint of the mass of an object

conversion — the process of changing from one form to another

energy — the ability to do work and overcome resistance friction — the resistance to motion of surfaces that touch

friction — the resistance to motion of surfaces that touch

gravity — a basic force pulling all objects toward one another — the greater the mass of an object, the greater that gravity affects it

inertia — the tendency of matter to resist a change in motion

lift — a force that moves an object upward

momentum — a force with which an object moves against resistance, equal to the product of its mass and velocity

pressure — force applied to a unit area, measured in terms of pounds per square inch (psi)

static electricity — a charge that builds up when electrons (very small particles that our eyes can't see) are moved from one surface to another

surface tension — a force at the surface of any liquid due to molecules being pulled closer together

velocity — speed with which an object is moving in a given direction